# What Is Soil?

Phillip Simpson

## Contents

# What Is Soil?

Go outside and look at the ground under your feet.

You will see that the ground is made up of many things. **Soil** is one of those things on the ground.

But what is soil and how is it formed?

Soil is the thin layer of ground on the surface of Earth.

Plants need to grow in soil.
They get food and water from the soil,
through their roots.

Soil can be all kinds of colours and grain sizes.

Soil colours can be black, brown, white, grey, yellow or red.

## How Is Soil Formed?

Soil is formed in many ways.

There are very tiny bits of rock in soil.

These tiny bits of rock have been broken down over many years by rain and wind.

Plants and animals that have died are an important part of soil.

Animals and plants die every day.

Animals and plants die on the ground most of the time. After they die, animals and plants break down to form part of the soil.

The dead plants and animals make very good soil. This soil is called **humus**. Humus is a soft, dark soil.

Plants grow strong and healthy in humus.

A plant grows well in humus.

Soil is formed in layers.

The layer below the humus is called **topsoil**. Topsoil is made up of **clay** and **sand**. The clay and sand in topsoil have small grains.

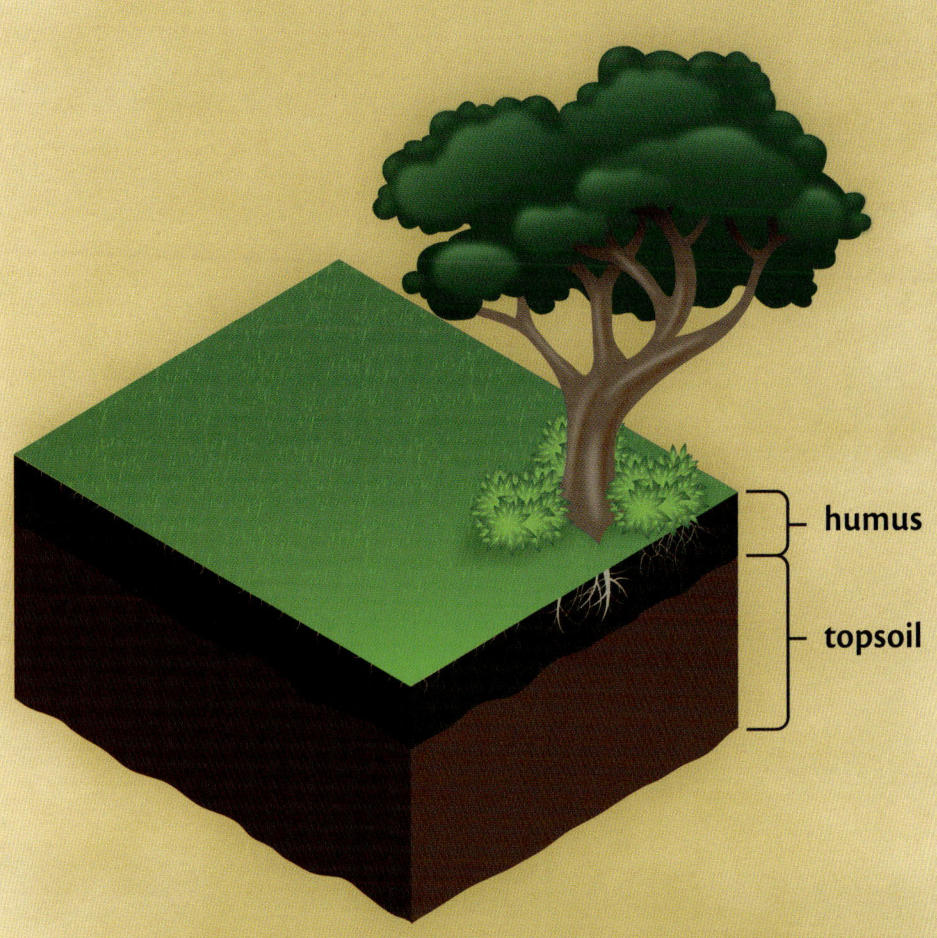

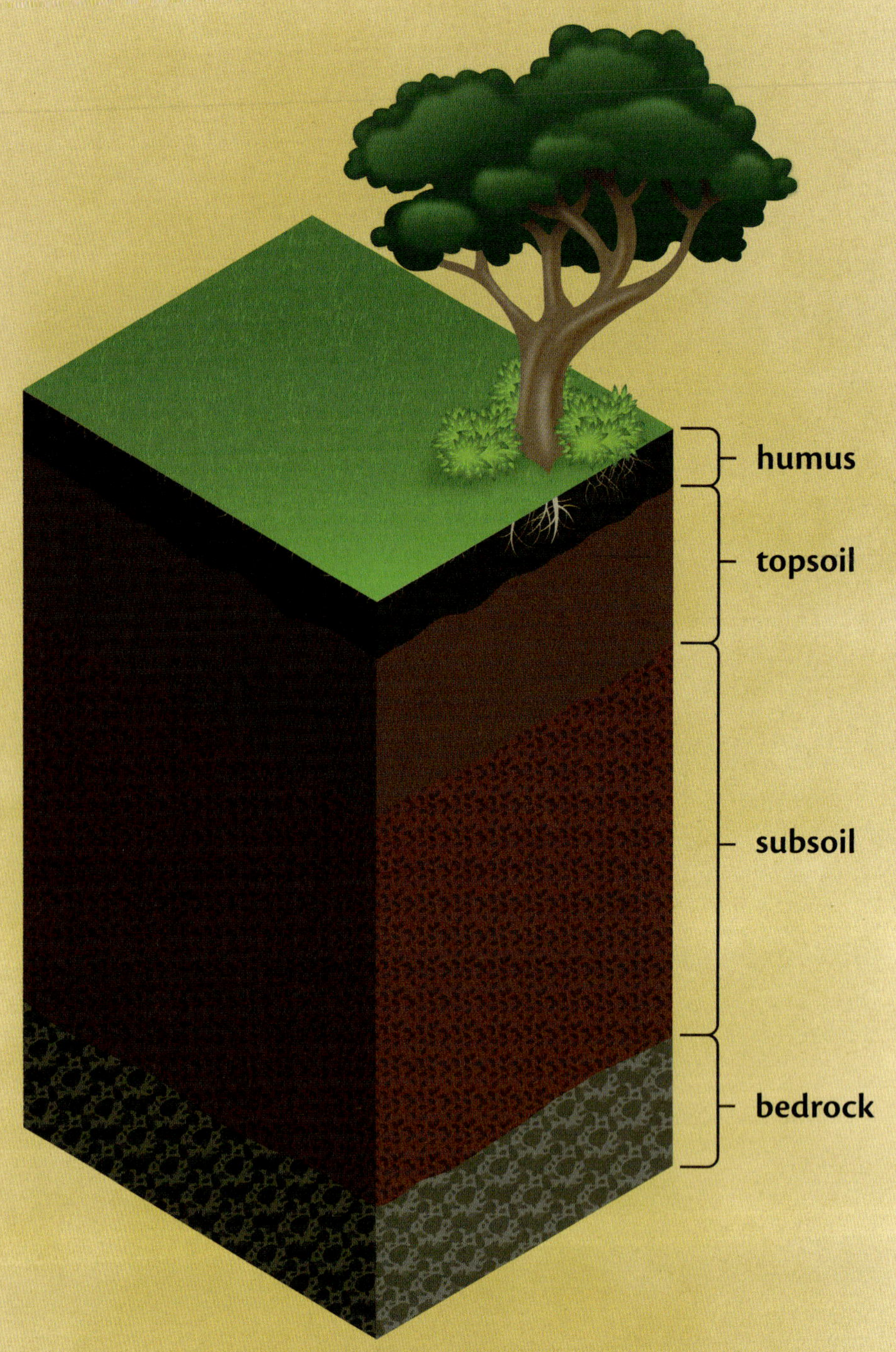
humus
topsoil
subsoil
bedrock

There is a layer of soil underneath the topsoil.
This layer is called **subsoil**.

Subsoil has larger grains and less humus than topsoil.
Pebbles and gravel are often found in the subsoil.

The layer below the subsoil is made of rock.
This layer is called **bedrock**.

Bedrock is made up of many kinds of rock.
It breaks down into smaller pieces over many years.

## How Do We Use Soil?

The pebbles and gravel found in soil are used to make many things.

Some buildings are made from pebbles and gravel. Many roads are made from gravel.

Soil sometimes has grains that are very small.
These grains are sand or clay.

Sand is very fine.
There is lots of sand at the beach.
Water passes through sand very quickly.

plants growing in sandy soil

Sandy soil is often loose and soft. The roots of trees and other plants grow well in sandy soil.

People make glass from sand.
The sand is heated,
so that it melts and turns into glass.

Glass can be used to make windows and bottles.

People who make glass from sand are called glass-blowers.

Another kind of soil is clay.
Clay is very thick.

Sometimes, clay is used to build mud-brick houses.

Clay can be used to make pots, too.
Clay has a lot more water in it than other kinds of soil.

This house is made out of clay bricks.

Clay is used in pottery.

Most plants do not grow well in clay.

Wet clay is thick and heavy.
Dry clay is very hard.
The roots of plants cannot grow in wet clay or dry clay.

**wet clay**

**dry clay**

People need to eat food every day.
Most of the food people eat
is grown in soil.

People need to be safe every day.
Many houses and roads are built with soil.

Soil is very important.

# Glossary

**bedrock** *(noun)* the bottom layer of soil, made up of pieces of rock

**clay** *(noun)* a thick, heavy soil

**humus** *(noun)* the top layer of soil, made from dead plants and animals

**sand** *(noun)* a light, fine soil

**soil** *(noun)* the thin top layer of Earth's surface

**subsoil** *(noun)* the layer of soil underneath the topsoil, made up of pebbles and gravel

**topsoil** *(noun)* the layer of soil below humus, made of clay and sand